THE WIT OF IRISH CONVERSATION

THE AUTHOR

TADHG HAYES was born in 1969 and lives in County Kerry where he works as a tour guide in Killarney National Park. There he meets and educates thousands of tourists in the delicate art of Irish conversation. Tadhg is single but hopeful.

The Wit of Irish Conversation

TADHG HAYES

Illustrated by Terry Willers

THE O'BRIEN PRESS
DUBLIN

This edition published 2001 by The O'Brien Press Ltd.,
20 Victoria Road, Dublin 6, Ireland.
Tel: +353 1 4923333; Fax: +353 1 4922777
E-mail: books@obrien.ie
Website: www.obrien.ie
First published 1997 by The O'Brien Press.
Reprinted 1998.
Originally published as *Gift of the Gab,* 1996, by GAB Publications.

ISBN: 0-86278-517-0

Copyright for text © Tadhg Hayes
Copyright for typesetting, layout, illustrations, design © The O'Brien Press Ltd.

All rights reserved. No part of this publication may be reproduced
or utilised in any form or by any means, electronic or mechanical, including
photocopying, recording or in any information storage and retrieval system,
without permission in writing from the publisher.

British Library Cataloguing-in-Publication Data
A catalogue record for this title is available from the British Library

3 4 5 6 7 8 9 10
01 02 03 04 05 06 07

Editing, typsetting, layout and design: The O'Brien Press Ltd.
Illustrations: Terry Willers
Colour separations: C&A Print Services Ltd.
Printing: The Guernsey Press Ltd.

Acknowledgements

We wish to thank all the staff at the bank we robbed in order to finance this book. Its completion is due in no small way to your co-operation.
We also wish to thank the following for their assistance and help to us while carrying out the raid:

Mama Hayes:	Safe House
Séan & Cathy:	Back-Up & Support
Hayes Mafia:	
Mícheál:	Driver
Maureen:	Maps
Siobhán:	Bank Robber # 1
Kieran:	Bank Robber # 2
Liam:	Bank Robber # 3
Breda:	Bank Robber # 4
Tomás:	Balaclavas
Pauline:	Moustaches
Caitríona:	Liquid Refreshments
Anthony:	Bullet Removal
Eibhlín:	Inside Intelligence
Jens:	Get-Away Car
Martin:	Bank Layout
Peter:	Heavy Artillery & Tanks
Bachem Fine Art Society:	Fake I.D.s

Also: Maura, Mary, Steve, Phillippe, Ann, Pierrette, Paulette, Trevor, Ger, Michelle, Aisling, Thomas, Cáit, Nell, John, Kieran Furey, Bernard Neary, the Muckross and Ross Castle Guides, Bob, David & Georgia

The money from the raid was laundered in Jack Sugrue's pub, Cromane.
Thanks, Jack!

Welcome to
The Wit of Irish Conversation

This is not just another Irish phrase book. This is the real thing: a practical user's manual to the art of conversation, Irish style, with lashings of words, phrases and sound advice.

Our aim in this course is to get you talking, not just because you want something, but for the pure pleasure of it. Talk is cheap, a great form of entertainment and by far the best way of getting to know the Irish.

This conversation guide uses a no-nonsense, subject by subject approach to learning the basics of Irish blarney. This allows you to dip in and find what you need when you need it. Countless hours of lively conversation are guaranteed. You will be a joy to listen to and a valuable companion to have in any situation.

On that note, let us begin and may you never be short of something to say!

CONTENTS

Part 1
Opening Lines
Greetings   9
The Weather   12
Health   17
Opening Questions   20
The Craic   23

Part 2
Cover-ups
The Poor Mouth   25
Excessive Modesty   28
Blarney   29

Part 3
Something for All Occasions
The Pub   33
Sport   41
Travel   45
Shopping   49
Visiting   52
Christenings, Weddings, Funerals   55
Awkward Situations   59

Part 4
Green, White, Orange – and Blue!
Fillers   62
Curses   63

Part 5
Parting Shots
Farewells   68
Congratulations   69
Dictionary   71

PART 1

Opening Lines

GREETINGS

From the dreariest low budget hostel to the suave sophistication of the luxury hotel, you will find it stuck on the wall: Céad Míle Fáilte, the slogan proclaims "one hundred thousand welcomes to you".

Funny thing is it's true. That man you saw twitching his head was not laughing at some private joke, he was saying HELLO! Now that you know how to recognise a ready and willing companion, let the craic begin ...

Popular Greetings
How's the Craic?
How's the form?
How're ye keepin'?
How's it goin'?
How're the men?
How're ee, lads?
What way are you at all now?
How's she cuttin'?

Are you well? Yes? Then say:
Grand!
We're fine out!
Things could be a lot worse!
I'm spot on!
I'm tearing away!

On top of all the above is the rather devilish:
>An'ting strange?

to which one should respond:
>Divil a bit! (i.e. nothing at all)

If you're not very well or perhaps a little unwell try:
>I'm up in a heap!
>I'm not too good!
>I'm in 'n awful way!

Greetings when eating

No, this has nothing to do with saying "hello" with your mouth full. Instead, greet somebody else who is eating with:
>Is it going down well?

They are sure to respond in true *Céad Míle Fáilte* style:
>It hasn't come up yet anyway. Will ye have a bite t'eat yerself?

On accepting this kind offer explain:
>I'm starved with the hunger!
>I'm so hungry, I'd eat a scabby child's arse!
>I'd eat the back door buttered!

A member of the older generation may greet you with the rather beautiful:
>Much good may't do ye!

Sadly, this is extremely rare.

Greetings and Work

It was an old Irish custom to give any job well done a blessing called an *Abarta*. The exact reason for this has now been forgotten, but today, a token blessing is still very much in order, say:
>God bless the work! (traditional blessing)
>Ye're hard at it! (i.e. working hard!)

To which everyone will automatically respond:
>We're doin' a bit!

GREETINGS

fig 1   fig 2   fig 3

Head Salute

Before we conclude, let's work on your salute. This head movement is generally performed in conjunction with the spoken greeting. It serves a number of functions:

- It acts as a universal sign of friendship in Ireland.
- It alerts your companions to the fact that you've spoken (no small consideration in the noisy pub, club, or sports ground).
- It unblocks your ear passages and improves hearing.
- It can help you to relax.

Use the graphical illustration above to learn the salute.

You may need a mirror to follow the movements accurately.

Now that you've taken the plunge, you will need something to talk about. Generally, a new topic will present itself without you having to look too far. Talk about *The Weather*, *The Craic*, or your *Health*. If you feel that something is worth mentioning, share it with your companion(s).

Most importantly of all, relax and let it happen!

The Weather

The weather in Ireland is very changeable. It is as dramatic as it is newsworthy. What's more, it requires no introductions. Talk about it when and wherever you wish.

For ease of description, we have classified the weather into *Good*, *Bad*, and *Indifferent*, as follows:

Good Weather

All very good weather is termed "mighty" weather. "A mighty day" brings spells of sunshine and some degree of warmth. On days that fit this hazy definition, you should comment:

We're blessed with the fine weather!

Or indeed, you may choose from a wide variety of adjectives to extol the elements:

'Tis glorious!
'Tis marvellous altogether!
'Tis gorgeous weather we're having!
'Tis lovely!

A little less exquisite, but lovingly embraced all the same, is the "grand day". Saying:

'Tis a grand day!

expresses general satisfaction with the atmospheric conditions.
As you can imagine, "grand weather" is a very relative concept. A "grand summer's day" does not correlate with a "grand winter's day". Sometimes a qualification is called for. To do this, simply add:

For the time that's in it! (i.e. for the time of year.)

With this, the eternal optimist may justify praising even the worst winter's day.

Anything that is greatly praised is bound to be much maligned as well. Good weather is no exception. Far from being a bad thing, this tendency may discourage us blue-skinned natives from burning ourselves to a fine crisp on the first (and last) sunny day of summer. You too should join in this healthy evangelical activity. Always warn those you meet with:

We'll be burnt alive!
You'll be scalded!

Finally, the vagaries of the Irish weather dictate that any fine spell will be short-lived. To any positive comments, announce:

'Twill never last!

You will find, of course, that a bad summer is always inevitable. On any fine spring or summer's day, comment:

I s'pose this'll be our summer!

Bad Weather

Good weather is a rare enough occurrence in Ireland. Consequently, when the natives talk about the weather, assume that we are referring to the bad weather.

While bad weather is an important talking point, avoid watery phrases like:

The weather is bad! or

It's bad weather!

No marks will be gained by stating this all too depressing fact. Instead, your energies will be better spent commenting on the rain, cold, and wind that make the bad day unpleasant.

Rain

Many visitors to Ireland come from countries where the term "rain" is misunderstood. They foolishly believe that rain is a short-lived phenomenon, resulting in a watering of their back lawns. However, this is not rain. In Ireland, we call this a "passing shower". To understand rain you must imagine 100 passing showers in sequence so that one falls directly on top of the other.

Occasionally, there will be a hiccup in the running order, this is called a "dry spell", but for the most part the downpour continues unabated.

Now that you know what rain is, you will be eager to experience an authentic Irish downpour first hand. In preparation, we outline some facts and observations:

Rain is wet.
A wet day consisting of many extended showers is termed:
A dirty ould day!
The description:
Mouldy day!
is also used in this manner.
Rain falls in abundance from the sky. The falling action of rain is called "pissing". You may say:
'Tis pissing!
but equally acceptable are:
'Tis lashing!
'Tis flaking down out of the high heavens!
Rain falls from a canopy of clouds. Clouds block out the sunlight and make everything seem dull. For this reason, wet days are described as:
Wet 'n dreary!

Cold

Looking at the map, you'll spot the Emerald Isle floating between 50 and 60 degrees north latitude. It lies roughly the same distance from the equator as Moscow and Labrador. Because these places are very cold, it might also be deduced that Ireland is something of an icebox.

This is not so, however, for Ireland is bathed in the warm waters of the Gulf Stream. The tourist brochures are forever pushing this fact in an effort to convince the intrepid holidaymaker that our green isle is a place of tropical warmth and blue skies.

THE WEATHER

In reality, Ireland is neither Tahiti nor the North Pole, never an oven, rarely a freezer, but it can feel cold. This is due largely to the high humidity. While the rain may be warmer in summer, one is still liable to get wet; with this wetness comes a chill. If you do not counteract this chill, it will soak into your very bones. You're probably already familiar with the old nautical expression:

'Twould skin the balls off a brass monkey!

It's this same notion of penetrating cold that you will be required to describe. Try rolling the following off your tongue:

'Twould skin ye!
'Tis wicked cold!
I'm perished!

Wind

"If the Dutch lived in Ireland, 'twould be the richest country on earth. If the Irish lived in Holland, they would surely drown!"

Argue all you like about this aphorism, but one thing is for sure: If the Dutch lived in Ireland, the windmill would almost certainly overshadow the pint of Guinness as national emblem.

We strongly advise you to hold on to your cap and weigh the hem of your skirt down with stones. This fair land is a place of ruddy cheeks and wild windy bogs. We say:

'Tis savage!
The wind would cut through ye!

Not only that, but:

You'll be blown out of it if you're not careful!

While bad weather may consist of only one of the above, you are more likely to experience all three: rain, cold, and wind, simultaneously. This combination is suitably summed up with the remarks:

'Tis cat!
'Tis desperate!

The Indifferent

Falling between two stools is the "soft day". Characteristically mild and damp with a possible drizzle, the soft day is truly a bore. In response to this unhealthy state of affairs, you will often hear people sigh:

The day is only fit for a high stool! (i.e. the only place to be is in a

pub, sitting on a high stool with a drink in your grasp.)
Once inside the pub, and only then, should you get philosophical about the situation outside. Try:
Soft day, thank God!
As you'd expect, the "soft day" offers little fodder for a good chat – but never fear! Before long the sun will explode on the horizon, the wind will whip at your heels and there'll be lots more to say. Don't be afraid to get emotional: Exaggerate, if you feel so inclined (your companions will!). A "soft" morning will transform into a "mighty" afternoon or will alternatively convert into:
An absolute sickener!

Down on the Farm

This section would not be complete without a brief mention of the poor farmer, for s/he battles the elements every day in a struggle to

survive. No matter how bored you are with the topic, never assume that the feeling is mutual. How could it be, when life and limb depend on a dry summer or a mild winter!
When you spot a farmer in a field, lean over the fence and comment:

There's great growth there!
There's great drying there!
Or should you happen upon a pub full of hibernating farmers on a "wintry" day, join them and sympathetically condole:
'Tis a terrible bad day, the fields are swimmin'!
How's a wo/man suppose to work in this weather?

Health

There's nothing that people like more than talking about their hardships. Be honest! You love the attention, the sheer unadulterated indulgence of sharing your woes? Imagine lying in bed, with a Florence Nightingale look-alike constantly on the go, bringing hot whiskeys, flat 7-up, and buckets of sympathy, all because you're knocked out with a bad dose of the flu.

Health may be wealth, but the odd headache or cold will do no long-term damage. If anything, your runny nose will excite concern, and a lively discussion will ensue (the pleasure to be gained from this topic is proportional to the suffering described).

If ever you need a new topic of conversation, introduce a description of your personal state of health. Don't be shy, no one else is!

A–Z of Physical Ailments

ANAEMIA
S/he's looking shook!
S/he's the colour of death!

ARTHRITIS
I'm all aches 'n pains!
I'm as stiff as a poker!
I'm riddled with arthritis!

COLD
I'm smothered with a cold!

FRAILTY
You'd blow him/her away!

HEADACHE
I've a reeling in my head!

HIGH BLOOD PRESSURE
I've a meadhrán in me head! (pron. Meow-rawn)

INFLUENZA
I'm dying with the flu!

OPENING LINES

Poor health, generally, may be described by any of the following:
The health is very bad by her/him!
He'll never comb a grey hair!
He'll soon be a load for four! (i.e. carried by four pall bearers)
You're as pale as a ghost!
She's failing!

Mental Maladies

Mental maladies are equally topical, but you should be careful not to offend your companion with a brash, offensive remark about her/his own psychological wellbeing. You avoid this pitfall by directing your attention towards those who are out of hearing range.

Two categories of mental disorder are outlined below. The former, *Eccentricity*, should be taken with a pinch of salt. All it means is that the person under scrutiny is different (but "aren't we all", I hear you say!). The latter, *Depression*, is treated with utmost seriousness, so lose the smile when discussing it.

Eccentricity

S/he's quare in the head!
S/he's a quare hawk!
S/he's not all there!
S/he's not the full shilling!

Depression

S/he's very down in the mouth!
S/he's a sad poor ol' crathur!

Health Matters Discussed

When responding to any comments regarding a third party's state of health, it is wise to treat the remark with serious concern:
Is that the way?
Is that so?
No word of a lie?
Expressing sympathy in a one-to-one context will also convey your understanding:

HEALTH

'Tis an awful dose you have!
That flu is no joke!
You should be at home in bed for yerself!

Finally, the subject may be developed further by asking:
   Are you taking something for it?
No doubt, you will be able to recommend a cure if called on to do so.

Any of the above will elicit the generous concern of your audience and will, no doubt, prompt anecdotes in a similar vein. Once you have massaged your woes, it is normal to expand into new avenues of interest.
   Here we go!

OPENING QUESTIONS

In the opening stages of a conversation it is important to learn about your companions. Only then will you know what really interests them. You must enquire politely, yet insistently, into their backgrounds, and expect similar unbridled curiosity in return.

Where are you from?
This, the eternal question, will be asked countless times, in various forms:
> *You're not a local, I take it?*
> *You're not from around, are ye?*
> *You're new 'round these parts?*
> *Where ye from at all?*

Don't assume that an abrupt "yes" or "no" answer will do. One word replies are miserly and indicate an unwillingness to converse. Replace them with generous, well-rounded, statements instead.
To questions beginning:
> *You're not a ...?*

Reply:
> *Indeed, I am not!*

Likewise, those opened by:
> *Are you ...?*

Reply:
> *I am indeed!*

If your companion's assumption is untrue, simply use one of the above in reverse:
> *You're not a ...?*

Reply:
> *I am indeed!*

You may now inform the listener of your exact origins. Use the phrase:
> *I'm over from ...?*

But equally acceptable are:
> *I was born and reared in England!*
> *I was bred and buttered in Germany!*

OPENING QUESTIONS

Given your love of language, why not try turning one of the above on its head:

'Twas in Canada, I was born and reared! etc.

In return for your companion's interest, reward her/him with:

And where are ye from yerself?

The fact that each pocket of Ireland lays claim to its own unique accent makes this question as relevant to the native as to the visitor. The Irish resident will use "down from" and "up from" in the sense of "north" and "south" respectively. The Kerryman in Dublin says: "I'm up from the Kingdom!" i.e. Kerry, while the teacher working in Belfast goes "down" to visit her parents in Dublin at the weekend.

Visitors from far away places will add "of all places" to their response ending:

I'm from Zimbabwe, of all places!

but this little extra may also be used to give more punch and possibly uniqueness to your origins:

I'm from Australia, of all places!

I'm from two miles out the road, of all places!

Finally, the visitor to Ireland with Irish relatives should proclaim this fact loud and clear:

I wasn't born here myself, but my grandmother on my father's side was a Galway woman!

Why are you here?

Never ask this question directly as it is considered too forward. Skirt around the issue instead with:

You're around for a while, are ye?

You're around on a bit of a holiday, are ye?

These enquiries should be seen as general invitations to open up and talk about yourself. No specific information is being demanded. As before, begin your answer by either confirming, or denying, your companion's observation:

I am, indeed! (i.e. yes)

I'm not then! (i.e. no)

And continue with a vague reference to what your main concern is at that time, be it business or pleasure:

I'm over for the Craic!

OPENING LINES

I'm over for the fishing!
I'm down for a few rounds of golf!
I'm visiting the relations!
I'm doing a bit of work locally!

Other Questions

Should you find your companion stubbornly adept in the vagueness department, the following queries should be used:

What are ye doin' these times? (i.e. what are you working at now?)
What do ye do for a crust? (i.e. what do you do for a living?)
What's the Craic like 'round? (i.e. what's there to do in the area?)
You've done a fair share of travelling yerself, I'd say?
You're not Owen Mangan's son, are ye?

If all else fails, throw in a few phrases from *The Weather*.

Always get a better understanding of who your companion is. There is no need to be shy about asking. As you've seen, personal questions are rarely put in too forward a manner. If you do feel threatened or intimidated by certain enquiries, for whatever reason, excuse yourself momentarily. When you are out of your companion's view, steal a glance at the section entitled *Awkward Situations*.

THE CRAIC

The Craic is a commodity that you will meet sooner rather than later in Ireland. It refers to all aspects of one's social life, and can include everything from a day's work to a night in the pub.

To have Craic, you will need the following:
- One or more people,
- Interesting conversation,
- A generous mix of excitement and playfulness.
- An Irish accent and pint of stout/glass of whiskey, while not essential, may add a touch of authenticity to the experience.

Talking about the Craic

Most commonly, The Craic is used in greeting:
How's the Craic? (i.e. how's life treating you?)

OPENING LINES

In reply, choose any one of the following key words:
Gas! (good)
Mighty! (very good)
Unbelievable! (extremely good)
Poor! (bad)
Useless! (very bad)

Or simply moan:
There's no Craic!

Even more importantly, you may introduce a new topic of conversation by stating:
I had great Craic last night!

Your companion will follow this lead with suitable questioning:
What were ye at?
What were ye doin' with yerself?
Tell us what happened!

The Craic is directly linked to a mastery of blarney. Any companion who is a gifted conversationalist is described as "good", "gas", or "mighty" Craic!

If, on top of this, your companion exhibits odd or eccentric tendencies, call them:
Half Craiced!

or,
Mad Craic! (a condition that is no less desirable, and just as common)

PART 2

Cover-Ups

THE POOR MOUTH

The Poor or complaining *Mouth* dominates Irish conversation. It dictates that the rich are struggling, the poor are barely surviving, and those with nothing are heroes. Poor or not, everyone pretends to share the same bank balance:
I haven't a bob to call my own!
I'm just scrapin'!
I haven't a copper to my name!

But there is much more – for, in Irish blarney, what's good is bad, and what's bad is simply desperate. Rather than admit that you are well, instead, you are "only grand" or "only all right". Everyone will automatically concur that your situation is hopeless, with the words:
'Twill have to do!
There's no use in talking!

The Poor Mouth is present in almost every conversation in Ireland. See how positive is changed to negative:
It's good!
Becomes:
It's not too bad!
It's bad!
Becomes:
It's not too good!
S/he's old
Becomes:
S/he's no spring chicken!
He's young!
Becomes:
He's only a young fella!

COVER-UPS

Terrible as all this must seem, it is only a game. Don't be too gloomy. Remember, if everyone were happy, there would be very little to talk about. Finally, the undeclared game is won by the person who puts forward the most convincing personal state of poverty and decay.

The following guaranteed winners will raise a smile and never let you down.

You are being called
Are you there?
Response:
I'm here, all that's left of me!

Greetings
Are ye well?
Response:
I'm well, considering!
How's the form?
Response:
I'm on me last legs!

Compliment
You've done a great job!
Response:
'Twill have to do!

Observation
The game was brilliant!
Response:
'Twasn't too bad!

House call
Who's there?
Response:
'Tis only me!

COVER-UPS

EXCESSIVE MODESTY

Another institution of Irish conversation that is very much related to *The Poor Mouth* is *Excessive Modesty*. This custom demands that you belittle yourself, so that you appear more humble than you are.

When you are thanked for your efforts, always insist that:
 'Twas nothing! (i.e. I wasn't much use to ye)
On receiving further gratitude respond:
 No bother at all!
But graciously add:
 You're more than welcome!
In addition, every compliment should be accepted unwillingly.

Compliments
 The meal was very tasty!
Response:
 'Twas nothing too fancy!
 You played well!
Response:
 I did my best!
 You're looking great!
Response:
 'Tis the divil pulling me leg! (i.e. you're joking me)

One can never be too humble. Your companion must not feel inferior to you, or your abilities. The good thing about all of this is that the more you belittle yourself, the more compliments you will receive. Like *The Poor Mouth*, this is a game, but in this case you always win!

Blarney

Queen Elizabeth I invented the term "Blarney" back in the early 1600s. It seems that a certain Cute Hoor by the name of Cormac Mac Carthy was courting her at the time, in an effort to retain his position as head of the Mac Carthy clan.

The conflict resulted from their differing views on property rights. The Queen was attempting to enforce the old Norman view that all land was ultimately the property of the crown. Mac Carthy, on the other hand, followed the Gaelic belief that land belonged to the clan, and was to be held on their behalf by the

COVER-UPS

elected chieftain.

It was a catch 22 situation. If Mac Carthy ignored the Queen he was inviting trouble, while abandonment of the clan system was sure to evoke the wrath of his namesakes. Faced with the difficult choice of death or death, Mac Carthy decided to avoid the issue and resort to flattery and coaxing talk, i.e. "Blarney", to "get around" the Queen. That is why it's said that "he ran with the hare and ran with the hound!" He was at once a friend of the Queen and a friend of the clan, but above all else he was his own best friend – he retained his land!

The old Mac Carthy stronghold is Blarney Castle and that's where you'll find The Stone embedded under the battlements. They say that kissing it will reward you with "The Gift". No guarantees are given, but if you ask anyone who's done it, they'll reply:

Sure, what harm will it do?

The survival technique of old is now a customary activity. While you may not be dependent on your loquaciousness to stay alive, an ability to charm the pants off your companions will reward you with their friendship.

Increase your charm 100 percent, right now. Start using the expressions that follow in your speech. These may seem small and inconsequential but – believe us – they really work!

Right form of Address

Ideally, it is best to address persons by name, as this shows that your sole interest rests with them. Unfortunately, an individual's name will not always be at hand, so here is a selection of suitable alternatives:

MY DEAR MAN!/MY DEAR WOMAN!

To be used with friends and mere acquaintances alike. This address has a formal fatherly tone about it, so say it with a sparkle in the eye and a toss of the head, to show that no such relationship exists.

LIKE A GOOD FELLA/LIKE A GOOD WOMAN

Note that this is not simply "good fella" or "good woman". The "like" element is very important. On asking anybody to do anything for you,

always add the above as a form of "please". For example:
> Would ye ever get me a few messages, like a good fella?
> Can ye tell me where the toilets are, like a good woman?

THE LADS
Use in familiar talk to address two or more people you already know. The lads are not necessarily men, so feel free to apply this to any group, mixed or otherwise. One usually asks:
> How're ee, Lads?

or,
> Are the Lads around?

YER WAN/YER MAN
These act as general terms for "that woman" and "that man". Instead of saying "Look at that man", try:
> Look at yer man!

The tourist who requires a map will be advised that one may be bought from "yer wan" in the shop.

HIMSELF/HERSELF
Again, these addresses replace "that man" or "that woman", but in addition they carry the notion of special importance. "Himself" is not Joe Soap or John Doe: He is a character who has acquired seniority through sheer graft and effort. In a home, "Himself" will be the father or the most senior male, while "Herself" will be the mother or the most senior female.

Active Listening

Your chances of winning the speaker over are vastly improved when you show real interest in what s/he says. The speaker who is aware of your full attention, will also be willing to understand and concur with the sentiments that you express. This symbiotic relationship is achieved through active listening.

Active listening requires you to be sympathetic to the speaker's view-point and ready and willing to respond.

Because you are in the process of conversing with another, we will assume that you are sympathetic to the speaker's views. You now need to react verbally. A selection of highly effective responses are given:

DISBELIEF
Titillated by the speaker's news, you will burst out with:
> *Is that the way?*
> *Go 'way out o' that!*
> *You're havin' me on!*
> *Are ye codding me?* (i.e. joking me)

CONTINUE
Enraptured by the story line, you will beg for more:
> *Carry on, carry on!*
> *And what happened then?*

DIVINE PRAISE
Exalted by the scale of the revelation, you resort heavenward:
> *Well, Holy God!*
> *Glory be to God, isn't that marvellous!*

DIVINE PROTECTION
And finally, Divine Protection should be sought in response to any tragedy, however minor:
> *My house was burnt down!*

Response:
> *God between us and all harm!*
> *The bus was two hours late!*

Response:
> *God help us!*
> *My cat had kittens!*

Response:
> *Lord save us!*

PART 3

Something for All Occasions

THE PUB

Irish pubs, like American fast food joints, are to be found in every corner of the globe. All seek to create an atmosphere redolent of Ireland. Many succeed. Many more are kitsch, bastardised versions of the real thing.

It is widely accepted that drinking is synonymous with Ireland. Thoughts of this Soggy Green Isle conjure up images of debauchery and hangovers requiring hospital care. Ironically, the Irish do not drink anywhere near as much as has been purported. Average alcohol consumption is well below that of our European and American neighbours. Still, the myth persists, little aided by the fact that it's a great way of attracting tourists, half of whom are total alcoholics according to the statistics. Add to this the high international profile of Irish beverages, and you have a powerful image, beyond possible redress by these few lines.

Pub Culture

Drinking in Ireland is a very public hobby. It is done in the Public House, usually shortened to "The Pub". The pub is basically an extension of home, and supports a wide range of homely activities such as eating, drinking, dancing and even sleeping. Therefore, it would be incorrect to assume that the pub exists solely to facilitate the rapid disposal of unwanted brain cells. On the contrary, it serves as a public amenity, arguably more important than any children's playground or public library. It is a resource shared by all, children included, and is a forum for discussions on every imaginable subject, from the earnest to the frivolous.

More importantly, a trip to the pub punctuates all social outings. It is this phenomenon that has given rise to the term "Pub Culture".

Given the importance of the pub in Irish life, the phrases that follow will initiate you into the practicalities of getting there, ordering a drink, and enjoying your drink.

Getting there

Invite a companion to the pub. This is a great sign of friendship and is easily done:
   Are ye on for a pint?
   Will ye go for a jar?
   Will we go for a few scoops?
Accept this kind offer with:
   Sure, what harm will it do!
   We'll go for "the one"! (not to be taken literally)
   A few pints wouldn't go astray at all!
Alternatively, venture into the pub alone, sit at the counter and order a drink. By placing yourself in this highly visible spot, you are expressing your openness to converse, a fact that will not be lost on your fellow drinkers.

Ordering a drink

If you are accompanied to the pub by a companion(s), it is good practice to buy a round of drinks for both them and yourself. They, in turn, will buy you a drink. Ask:
   What are ye having?
   Will ye have a pint? (of stout)
In some cases you may wish to decline the offer of alcohol. The car driver will say:
   I'm on the dry!
but will, no doubt, have a "Mineral" (i.e. soda) instead. You bridge the interval between drinks with:
   Will ye go again?
If further prompting is required add:
   A bird with one wing can't fly!
   'Tis as well to hang for a sheep as for a lamb!

Enjoying your drink

Ask your companions if they are happy with their drink:
How's that for ye?
How's that goin' down?
The happy drinker will respond:
I'm well pleased with it!
'Tis powerful stuff!

Occasionally, a pint of stout will not meet the high standards required of it (by the experienced drinker). This type of drink is known as a "bad pint". If you are unsure about the merits of your pint of the Black Stuff, consult your companion. If you feel nauseated the following morning, blame it on the "bad pint". It is perfectly acceptable to explain your total lack of co-ordination with:
I had a bad pint last night!

Please note that the flashing of lights at the end of the night is not the result of some hallucinogenic property particular to Irish beer. Instead, it is an indication that "last drinks" are being served. This nightly event is met with a display of unbridled self-interest, with all sizes jockeying for attention at the bar. The chances of being served quickly at this stage are greatly improved if you have established a rapport with the bar person earlier in the night:
There'll be a fair share 'round later, I s'pose?

If politeness fails to furnish you with liquid refreshment, try standing on your toes and moan:
I'm dying with the thirst!

Responding to inebriation

It has been said that "a few drinks will do you no harm", but most will agree that "you wouldn't feel the best after a night on the tear". Nights of excess such as this are best compared to a marathon. A steady pace is required, particularly in the opening stages. Encourage your companion to avoid early burn-out with:
Ye better go aisy on the drink!

Unfortunately, even the best intentioned of us will "lose the run of ourselves at times". The concerned partner will offer suitable words of advice in such cases:
Steady yerself up!

Those who have been through the same experience in a previous life will decide that food is required:
'Tis time for soakage!

Categories of drinker

Of all the different categories of drinker, two are worthy of specific mention: those who "can hold their drink" (i.e. drink a great deal without falling down), and those who are "fond of the bottle". The "bottle" refers to alcohol that is drunk outside the purely sociable setting of the pub. This activity is frowned upon. In between these two extremes is the rather ambiguous:
He's a great man for the drink!
which basically means that he loves to drink.

Levels of intoxication

Finally, in the unlikely event that you will need to describe your condition, the following classifications, arranged in ascending levels of intoxication, may be useful:

Well on!
Full!
Well oiled!
Half pissed!
Pissed!
Rightly pissed!
Pissed as a coot!
Flootered!
Maggoty!
Airlocked!
Legless!
Langered!
Bolloxed!
Paralytic!
On the floor!

Popular Irish drinks

WHISKEY

Uisce Beatha (pron. Ish-ka Ba-ha) is what they called it in olden times. Then, it was anglicised to *Fuisce* (pron. Fish-ka). Now, we call it "Whiskey".

THE PUB

The story of the golden spirit in Ireland began over 1,000 years ago with the introduction of a distillation apparatus, called an alembic. At first, experimentation was confined to monasteries, but soon whiskey stills mushroomed in the homes of ordinary people across the land. The rest is history and the "Water of Life" (translation from Gaelic) hasn't stopped flowing since.

Today, you can choose from a range of Irish whiskies including Paddy, Power's, Bushmill's, and Jameson. Try drinking them neat or diluted with a little water as the purists do, and watch out for the bite: "like a candlelit procession going down the throat".

In contrast to Scotch whisky, the Irish is said to possess a milder and altogether more delicate flavour. Its sweet taste contrasts nicely with the bitterness of stout. Both can be drunk together and are enjoyed all the more for it.

Ask for:
   A pint and a small one!

Alternatively, why not try a hot whiskey with the addition of lemon, cloves, brown sugar, and boiling water; or an Irish coffee with all the goodness of black coffee, sugar, and whiskey – mixed together and topped off with cream.

STOUT

Stout is arguably the unofficial emblem of Ireland. Yet, this drink, made from roasted barley, began life in 18th-century London where its popularity amongst the porters of Billingsgate and Covent Garden earned it the name Porter. The appearance of Porter in Dublin in the 1760s, led Arthur Guinness to have a go at making this new beer himself. So successful were his attempts that by the 1820s Guinness Porter was being enjoyed across the world.

The recession that followed the Napoleonic wars resulted in many brewers diluting their beers. Contrary to this popular trend, the 2nd Arthur Guinness strengthened his Porter and labelled it Extra Stout. Over the years, this Extra Stout has become synonymous with Ireland. Now shortened to "Stout", you will find it on sale from different companies, under a variety of brand names including Murphy's, Beamish, and, of course, Guinness. Each requires the same care when being pulled (i.e. poured) – slowly and in stages, in order to create a good creamy head.

It is said that the taste of a particular stout varies considerably from pub to pub. Indeed, different taps within the one pub may produce stouts of contrasting flavour. You have been warned! The merits of a good pint have given rise to many hours of heated discussion in public houses the length and breadth of Ireland. As you've probably guessed, Stout is sure to loosen your tongue.

POTEEN

Poteen is the Irish version of Moonshine or Mountain Dew. In other words, it's very illegal but no less popular as a result. You will be offered a glass of the *Crathur* (pron. Kray-thur) in the most unlikely of places, but beware – it will leave you numb, sore and sorry. This drink is definitely not for the faint-hearted!

Sport

Once a sporting event grabs the popular imagination in Ireland, the country goes wild. There is no escaping it. Every move in the game is discussed, every action is debated, and the question on everybody's lips is "Were ye at the match?"

Sport is serious business, for there is pride at stake. While all hope to win, most will admit, privately at least, that it's the taking part that counts. You too will be expected to join in the fun. Even if you've never "kicked a ball" or "pucked a sliotar", your comments and observations will be more than welcome.

Rather than sending you in with the natives without the basic skills necessary to survive, we will give a quick outline of the games you may be unfamiliar with.

Gaelic games

HURLING

This game dates back to pre-Christian times. It is played with a stick called a "hurley". The hurley is waist-high(ish), with the striking end curved broadly like a hockey stick. The hurley "pucks" (i.e. hits), a small leather ball called a "*sliotar*", the aim being to drive the *sliotar* into the opponents' goal.

GAELIC FOOTBALL

Another ball game this, dating back to the early 1500s. Gaelic football is, as the name suggests, played with the feet rather than a hurley. Again, the object of the game is to get the ball into the opponents' goal. Gaelic football, or "football" as it's generally known, involves lots of jumping, skipping, hopping and running. It's fun to watch: there's plenty of shouting, and action galore.

ABOUT HURLING AND FOOTBALL

- There are fifteen players on each of the opposing teams.
- The football or *sliotar* may be carried in the hand for no more than four steps.
- The ball may travel along the ground, up in the air, or anywhere in between.
- There is no offside as in soccer. The players can lob the ball in towards the opponents' goal at any time, so danger is never far away!

The same goal is used for football and hurling. It's in the shape of an "H". Kicking or pucking the ball over the crossbar will reward you with one point. Hitting the ball under the crossbar will get a goal. Even if you forget the rules of the game, remember that one goal is equal to three points.

HORSE RACING

Ireland boasts 15,000 race horses and every year well over 250 race meetings are held in tracks countrywide. Highlights include the Irish Derby, which takes place on the last Sunday of June or the first Sunday of July, and the Irish Grand National, held at Fairyhouse on Easter Monday. The race meeting is a great occasion for a gamble. When in Ireland, don't miss this important social highlight. Bring plenty of cash and this conversation guide. Heart-stopping excitement lies in store!

OTHER SPORTS TO WATCH OUT FOR

Soccer: ask about Saint Jack, the ex-manager of the Irish soccer team and his band of globe-trotting supporters!
Road Bowls: rolling a ball along a road).
Handball: (racquetball played with the hand.
Sheaf Tossing: throwing bundles of straw over a bar.
Sheep Dog Trials: sheep dogs gathering sheep into pens.
Rowing: weekly regattas on summer Sundays.

SPORT

What to say

EXPRESSIONS OF ENCOURAGEMENT
The following should be shouted when watching a sport live or on TV:
   Up ye boyo!
   Give it a lash!
   We'll show yee yet!

EXPRESSIONS OF ADVICE
(Remember that advice is always needed!)
> *Mark yer man!*
> *Lob it in!*
> *Watch the ball!*
> *On yer bike!* (i.e. get busy)
> *Come back, come back!* (i.e. retreat)
> *Get up, get up!* (i.e. attack)

EXPRESSIONS OF FRUSTRATION
> *What're ye at, ye lazy fecker?*
> *What's s/he at?* (i.e. what's s/he doing?)
> *Are ye goin' to play or what?*
> *Take him/her out of it!*
> *What the divil are ye at?*

In the inevitable post-match discussion always admit:
> *I'm hoarse from shouting!*

Of course, you will congratulate the team victors:
> *Yee gave 'em a roasting!*
> *Yee threshed 'em!*
> *Yee gave 'em a right beating!*

Specific players may be singled out for their superb performance:
> *He's a knacky young fella!*
> *S/he's a powerful player!*

While the champions are always heroes, the losers in Ireland never actually lose. Instead, they are merely victims of circumstance:
> *It's a wonder yee didn't win!*
> *Sure, the wind was against yee in the first half and the sun was in yer eyes for the second!*
> *Yee were badly stuck with Johnny going off injured 'n all!*
> *The ref was against yee!*
> *If ye played 'em again, I bet ye yee'd beat 'em!*

TRAVEL

Warning: Don't underestimate the challenge of travelling around the Emerald Isle! You may imagine that the small blob of green is barely able to support a cluster of pubs, two cows, a sheep, and a strip of bog (i.e. the airstrip); but don't be fooled!

Ireland is the 16th largest island on Earth. Therefore, your mode of transport requires serious consideration before you set off with your excitable husband, five pubescent teenagers, and dog in tow.

The Car

The car is the preferred means of travel of those who are "mad for road" (i.e. who love driving). These people enjoy the freedom of going wherever they choose, when they please. On the other hand, some find the act of controlling a car excessively demanding. These people "make no hand" of driving. If you fit this latter category, we strongly advise you make the most of the public transport system.

The decision to rent, borrow, or steal a car will be influenced by the following raw data:

HAZARDOUS OBSTACLES

Cows and sheep are hazardous obstacles:
 Avoid them!

IRISH DRIVERS

Another animal that poses a potential danger is "the Irish Driver". Two types have been identified: those who drive fast, and those who drive very fast (considering the state of the roads). The fast driver is known to:

 Boot it along the road

while the very fast driver:

 Gives her holly (her refers to the car)

In practice, both press hard on the accelerator. This invariably results in their cars "tearing along the road" at violent speeds.

In most situations, you may ignore the Irish driver. However, should you discover one of these speed freaks "up yer arse" (i.e. following too closely behind), slow your vehicle, while keeping well in to the fence (on the left, of course). This will allow the car behind to overtake you.

If, for some unimaginable reason, you find yourself sitting in a car that is about to break the sound barrier, caution the driver with:

Go aisy! (pron. Ay-zee)

or,

Slow down or we'll be kilt!

GETTING LOST

The map you buy looks nice and has the word "Ireland" printed on the plastic holder, but you still get lost! Let's face facts! Maps don't work, never have worked, and never will work, when you hold them upside down. Assuming that losing your way is a 100% certainty – which it is – you must seek advice as the first symptoms of disorientation emerge.

Advice should be sought from a native who will "put you right" when called on to do so. Rather than use road numbers, the native will focus on the name of your destination. Instead of driving on the N8 from Cork to Dublin, you are on "the Dublin road".

DRIVING ETIQUETTE

Despite the inherent risks involved in motorised transport, you will generally find that your fellow road users are courteous and friendly. This warm rapport is communicated by saluting other drivers or pedestrians with a finger raised over the steering wheel. You don't have to know someone to salute them. In country areas, you should salute every car or pedestrian that you meet.

BUYING FUEL

On stopping for petrol, ask for a "fiver's worth", "tenner's worth", or "twenty quid's worth". If asked how the car is running, say that you're pleased with its performance:

There's a powerful engine in her!
She's grand!
There's a grand chassis in her!

Or, if the vehicle fails to meet the high performance that you require:

She's a crock of an oul' car!
She's a right oul' banger!
She's banjaxed! (i.e. there's something wrong with the car)

CAR TROUBLE

If you have mechanical trouble, Don't Panic! The garage is an ideal place to strike up a conversation. You'll hear lots of talk about:
The ould engine
Ould brakes
Ould lights
In fact, every part of the car will take on some historical significance. Rise to the occasion! Throw in a few "ould" words yourself!

SOMETHING FOR ALL OCCASIONS

Shanks' Mare

A different experience entirely, and possibly more conducive to meeting companions for a chat, is travelling on "Shanks' mare" (i.e. on foot). This eco-friendly alternative gives you the liberty to create your own schedules, follow quiet country "boreens", and climb over "ditches" into landscapes unseen from the road. Incidentally, the word "ditch" is used to describe a fence, while "dike" is the term used to describe a drain.

High Nelly

You don't see many of them around nowadays, having been superseded by mountain bikes in the rental business. If you come across one of these heavy black bikes, jump on it without hesitation. The experience of luxuriating in the wide saddle is never forgotten.

By the way, riding is normally considered a sexual activity in Ireland. Instead of announcing that you went for a ride (on your bike), say:

I went for a cycle!

Finally, remember to salute the people who you pass on route with:

Grand weather!

SHOPPING

Shopping is called "Doing the messages". Before you depart for the grocery store (i.e. the shop), always ask:

Are there any messages you'd like me to get?

Do you want any messages?

In return you will be asked to get a few things (if it's not an inconvenience).

I've a few messages there ye might get me, if ye wouldn't mind!

Would I be putting ye out of yer way if I asked ye to get me ...?

Could I ever trouble ye to pick up a few messages on yer way?

At the shop counter, the assistant will enquire if you are being served, with:

Are ye all right there?

Are ye okay there?

Watch out! Some people mistake this enquiry for "Are you well?" If you have already been served, reply:

I'm grand!

or,

I'm fine out!

Otherwise, humbly ask for what you want, as if a favour is being sought:

Could I ever have ... if it wouldn't be too much trouble?

Can I have ... if you wouldn't mind?

"I" is often replaced with "Us" in such cases. If you are purchasing something small and insignificant try:

Give us a box of matches!

Give us a bar of chocolate!

The assistant now places your purchases on the counter and again asks:

All right now?

Is that okay?

As you turn on your heels to depart chirp "Good luck", and off you go. In keeping with the fact that you are asking a favour of the shop assistant, it is usual to explain why you so desperately need what you're buying. To guide you, some obvious reasons are given:

Don't buy potatoes, buy:

Spuds for the dinner!
Don't buy cheese, buy:
A few slices of cheese for a sandwich!
Don't buy tea, buy:
A grain of tea for the breakfast!

Customer service

Ireland is no paragon of virtue when it comes to customer service. It can be slow, sloppy, and erratic at times, much to the chagrin of the customer. That said, what may be lacking in efficiency is compensated for by the friendly reception that one generally receives. While Ireland may be a small, open-market economy, certain fundamentals of modern capitalism appear to be less engrained here than elsewhere. For one thing, the customer is not always king. Argue this fact if you like, by saying that the customer is the lifeblood of all transactions;

SHOPPING

nonetheless, casual observation shows the Irish customer to be humble, self effacing, with an outward reluctance to trouble the shop assistant with his or her demands. It appears, on the surface at least, that the average shopper is relatively shy, secretive, and lacking the confidence to demand the best for his or her money.

That said, looks can be deceiving, for the Irish shopper is a more sophisticated kettle of fish than is often thought. While the average customer may accept sub-standard service without complaining, it will only happen once. In Ireland if you don't like the treatment you receive, you don't go back to the same outlet a second time. What's more, it is normal to tell your friends of your bad experience, resulting in a poisoning of customer goodwill, and a possible demise of the premises concerned.

This behaviour begs the question "why?". Why not complain directly to your tormentors? Explanations vary, but it probably has to do with the Irish disdain for direct confrontation. Irish people do not like to display the full spectrum of their emotions in public. Nor do we react well to direct criticism. Anger on behalf of the consumer is normally met with mockery, as if to say: "Who the hell do you think you are?"

If you do need to complain, do so in a non-confrontational manner. Always be polite and deliberate, making sure to explain that it is the food/drink, etc., which fails to impress, and not the provider of this refreshment. Alternatively, in the more likely event of wanting to compliment the server, you can expect a response similar to those given in the *Excessive Modesty* section.

VISITING

The following points should be borne in mind when visiting an Irish home.

Watch out for the dog!
Even though you may have been assured in advance that "the dog won't go near ye", this guarantee should not be taken literally. If in doubt, you may wish to "peg a stone" in the general direction of the dog (just to scare it). Whatever your strategy, we strongly advise a consultation with the post wo/man in advance.

When a visitor calls, invite them in:
Come in for yerself!
Come in out of the cold, you'll be perished!
Come in out of the rain, you'll be drowned!
Come in an' take the weight off yer feet!
Come in 'til I talk to ye!

Rebuke a hurried caller with:
Take it easy, what's yer rush?
What's yer hurry?
What rush are ye in?
Come in for a minute!

On entering the house the electric kettle is "thrown on" (filled with water and switched on) for tea and the visitor is ordered to:
Sit yerself down!
Sit down there for yerself! Plank yerself down there by the fire! (pointing)

Hospitality in the home is not an act of kindness; it is a duty. The real objective of every host(ess) is to ply the visitor with food, drink and certain socially accepted drugs. The visitor's task, on the other hand, is to resist these temptations, albeit unsuccessfully.

The Irish are the greatest tea-drinkers in the world with the result that home visits always turn into long tea-drinking sessions. Tea is a diuretic, so remember to pick up your dirty underwear from the bathroom floor before the guests arrive.

When offering food and drink, a host should adhere to the proverb: 'Will' was never a good fellow! Instead of asking:
Will you have something?

VISITING

the gracious host will simply place the food and drink before the guest. The chance of a refusal will be greatly reduced as a result.
Use an order:

SOMETHING FOR ALL OCCASIONS

You'll have a drop of tea!
You'll have a bite to eat!

Or, try the old English word "sup" (i.e. a mouthful):

You'll have a sup of tea!

While these offers may be enticing, it is normal to test your host's generosity before accepting any food or drink.

If tempted with anything, always refuse it first time in the knowledge that a second overture will come (if the host really wishes you to have it). If another offer does not come, you must assume that the host was merely being polite, rather than generous.

Decline all offers first time:

Don't go to any trouble for me!
I won't be putting ye out at all!
I won't be staying long!
I'm just up from the table this minute! (i.e. I've just eaten)

A good host will wave these protests aside:

I shouldn't have asked ye at all, only given it to ye!
It's made now so ye may's well have it!
I'll forget I ever asked ye!

If the guest still declines the offer, try a different approach:

Maybe you'd prefer something stronger?
Do you take a drop? (of something stronger)
Maybe you're a coffee wo/man?

And if all else fails:

You'll have something!

The easiest thing to do at this stage is to accept. Choose your fare from what has been offered:

I'll have a small drop of ...!
I'll have whatever you're having yerself!
Only if you're having one yerself!

And add:

You're an awful wo/man!

This is an admission that the host has won your respect.

Christenings, Weddings, Funerals ...

Certain events such as *Christenings*, *Weddings*, and *Funerals*, hold a deep significance for all of us. Times like these call for special words. We have provided the following list to guide and inspire.

Christenings

On seeing a baby, massage the parents' vanity:
- *He's the spit of his father!*
- *He's a chip off the old block!*
- *She's the head cut off her mother!*
- *She's her mother's daughter!* (i.e. looks like her mother)

SOMETHING FOR ALL OCCASIONS

The sight of such a small human being may also evoke your tender affection:
S/he's a little dote!
Would ye look at the little smile by him/her!
Or, you may simply admire the miracle of childbirth:
S/he's fine 'n big!

Happy Birthday

"Happy" and "birthday" are two words that stand awkwardly side by side, for in truth the birthday is a time of introspection: "Where am I goin'?", "Where is time disappearin' to?", etc. In keeping with the philosophical state of the birthday person comment:
The years don't be long passin'!
You're shovin' on!
If it is your birthday respond:
I'm not getting any younger!
And to this, the kind observer will reply:
You'll be dancin' on my grave yet!
Ye don't look a day past ... (choose an appropriate age)
As in certain other parts, it is normal to give the "bumps" to the younger person. All four limbs are caught, stretched, and the poor unfortunate is catapulted up and down for the number of years in question. There are moves afoot to ban this activity because it frequently leads to injury. Before you decide to inform your companions of the momentous occasion, consider the full consequences of doing so.

Accidents

The irony of Irish conversation is that the joyous occasion is often seen in an almost negative light, while the unfortunate incident is usually viewed encouragingly. Always console the victim by giving a positive perspective on the accident:
It could happen to a bishop!
You could be dead and then where would you be?
It could be an awful lot worse!

Examinations
Life is full of little tests. Express your confidence in your companion's ability with:
> They'll be no trouble to ye!
> You'll fly through them!
> They won't be a bother to ye!

Engagement
The engagement begins the countdown to the wedding. Acknowledge this fact with the usual phrases heard everywhere:
> The big day won't be long comin'!
> Have yee a date set?

If the date is uncertain, answer "no" to the latter adding:
> But you'll be the first to know!

Weddings
The Irish wedding is "A day out" or a social highlight as in most other places. It is a time for renewing old acquaintances:
> What are ye at now?

And gathering useful information:
> Who's yer wan?

Furthermore, it's a great time for a blather, a few drinks, a song and a dance. If, having exhausted all the alternatives, you suddenly run out of something to say, make a polite reference to the marriage along the lines of:
> Isn't it great for them all the same!
> They've got it all before them!

What is actually before them is anyone's guess, so it's best not to specify!

Break-up or Divorce
Again, words of consolation are called for. Try:
> There are as good fish in the sea as ever were caught!
> Aren't ye better off without him/or her!
> S/he's a load off anyone's back!
> 'Twas the children I was worried about! (i.e. they're better off now)

At times, efforts will be made to comfort you with:
> *I knew s/he was trouble, the minute I saw her/him!*
> *Sure, what more could you expect from the likes of him/her!*

Or, if your emotions are that way inclined, choose a suitable description of your ex-partner from the dictionary at the back of this guide. Those derived from Gaelic are particularly vivid.

Funerals

The funeral has the added attraction over other gatherings in that it is totally spontaneous. There is usually a subdued carnival atmosphere, once one is not directly related to the deceased. When the talk turns towards the departed soul, you will be expected to compensate for your earlier festive mood with words of praise:
> *S/he was a lovely wo/man!*
> *Sure, s/he never harmed anyone!*

Deep human affection and regret should also be offered up in compensatory tones. Some examples:
> *The Lord have mercy on him/her!*
> *May God rest him/her!*
> *God be with him/her!*
> *S/he went very sudden!*
> *S/he's in good hands now!*
> *They won't know where they are without him/her!*
> *There won't be a dry eye after him/her!*

Awkward Situations!

Despite your keenness to converse, not everyone needs to know all your business. Use your own discretion in avoiding areas that you consider too personal. This is easily done. If, for example, you do not want to disclose your age when asked, avoid the question by asking another one: "What age would you say I am?" or "Hazard a guess yerself!" and the classic: "Why d'ya ask?"

A touch of wit will add further to your armoury:
  I've lost count!
  I've a few years left in me yet!
Always assure the listener that no offence has been taken by responding in a light-hearted way.

For improvers

At another level, the prudent management of your own business may be used to stimulate further interest and questioning. In this case you are not refusing to reward the curiosity of your partner. Instead, your aim is to milk this curiosity for all that it's worth. The easiest means of doing this is to add a touch of vagueness to your responses. A number of appropriate tools are outlined to help you do this.

BIT
The word "bit" infers a little and may be used to cloud what has been said. In the course of a chat, you should tell the listener that you do "a bit of this and a bit of that":
  I'm here on a bit of business!
  I'm taking a bit of a break!

EEN
The Gab has borrowed the suffix (word ending) "*een*" from Gaelic. "Een" conveys smallness and may be added to many words. "Bit" and "een" can be combined to form "biteen":
  I inherited a biteen of land lately!
Other words that may be added to include:
  Piece! (i.e. pieceen – small piece)
  Boy! (i.e. boyeen – small boy)
  Man! (i.e. maneen – one who strives towards manliness but fails due to age or lack of maturity)
  House! (i.e. housheen – small house)

ISH
Another suffix like "een", "ish" is used to express uncertainty:
  I'm sixtyish! (i.e. around sixty years old)
  I'm fairish! (i.e. fair to middling)
  I'm ish! (i.e. I don't know if I feel good or bad)
  The towel is dryish! (i.e. fairly dry)

The above tools may encourage further interest from your companion. When you do uncover an area of interest, make the most of it to bring pleasure to all concerned.

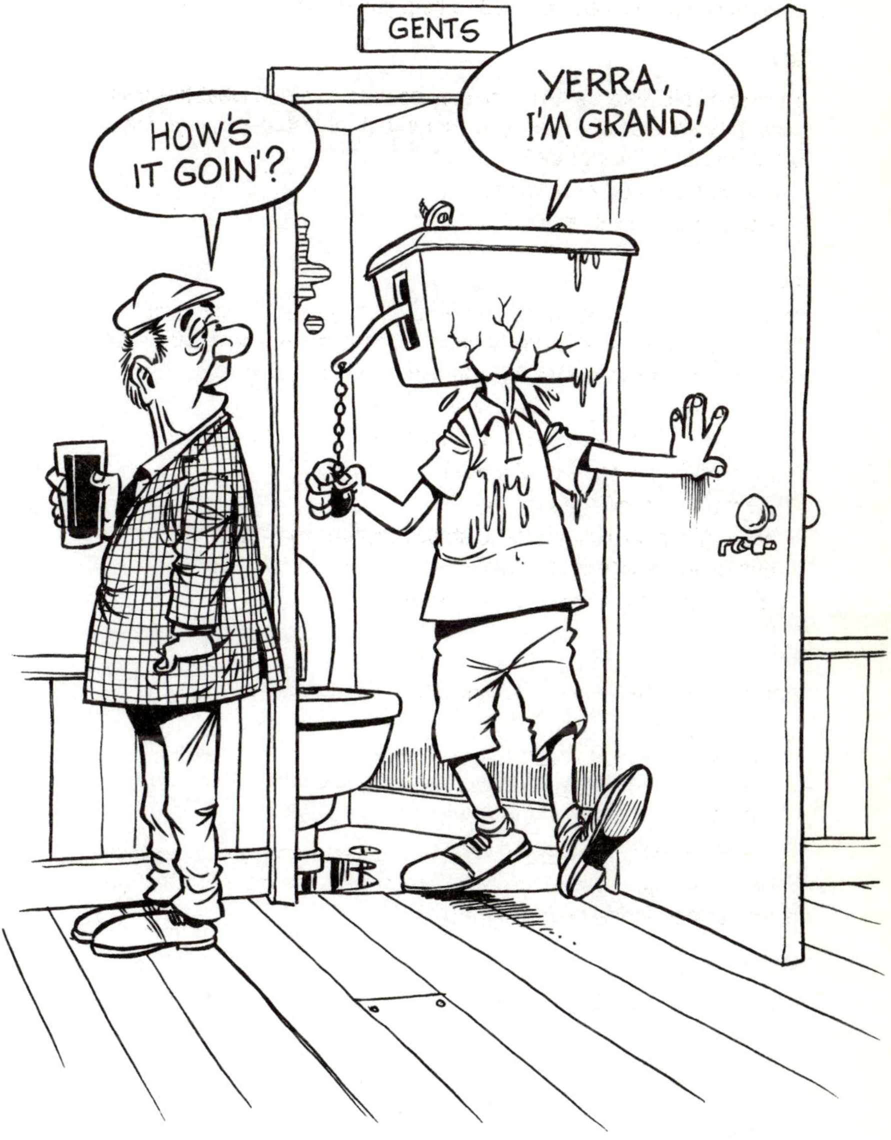
GENTS
HOW'S IT GOIN'?
YERRA, I'M GRAND!

PART 4

Green, White, Orange – and Blue!

FILLERS

There are certain sounds that can be used to make your speech sound more authentic. Give the following an airing and see how you get on.

YERRA
"Yerra" has no specific meaning but it is used to buy time before responding. It is also used to express sympathy with the speaker's point of view. For example:
How's it goin'?
Respond:
Yerra, I'm grand!

SURE
Use this as an opener when responding to a statement. It acts as a mild rebuke, as if to say "Be sensible!", for example:
Close the door!
Respond:
Sure, I was going to close it anyway!

WISHA
Wisha is used like "Yerra" and is much more popular with the older generation:
Wisha, what good's the money if we don't have our health!
Or, to your companion's complaint of poor health, console with:
Wisha, you'll be right as rain in no time!

BEGOB/BEGOR

Use this one as an all-purpose mouthwash. It's basically a substitute word for a curse:

Did ye make the dinner?
Respond:
I did, Begob!
What time's it?
Respond:
Begor, it's five o clock!

CURSES

You will hear *Curses* and *Swear Words* aplenty in Ireland. It is a vice shared by all, from politician to priest, though some will deny it. Even devout old ladies, bathed in autumnal serenity, will tell you where to stick it if pushed too far.

Not all of the *Curses* and *Swear Words* that follow are suitable for polite usage. To satisfy the overwhelming desire to curse, without incurring the wrath of the listener, the Irish will frequently use a milder variation of the real thing. While the alternative may resemble the forbidden curse in sound, it lacks venom. Therefore you will get away with it in most situations.

Saying that, what follows should not be considered a dilution of the real thing.

Mild Imitations

FECK

Feck is obviously derived from the word "Fuck". "Feck off" said angrily means "Go away!" but it is fairly harmless, and more often than not is used to add drama to a conversation. For example, the surprise victory of France over Ireland in a golf tournament might be greeted with:

FECK OFF, ARE YE SERIOUS?

You will also note an abundance of so-called "feckers" roaming around the Irish countryside. These men are usually fairly harmless and should pose no real threat to your general safety.

SHITE

The word "shite" frequently replaces "shit" in Irish conversation. Persons prone to excessive exaggeration or whose arguments lack basis in fact are said to be "full of shite". Alternatively, since "*gob*" is the Gaelic word for "mouth", an individual who is full of shite may also be called a "gobshite".

ME ARSE

Since we've introduced the word "shite", it is only appropriate that "me arse" get a mention. "Me arse" is an addition you will often hear at a phrase ending. One might respond:

I went to work, me arse! (i.e. Of course, I didn't go to work!)

Also to be heard is:

I couldn't bother me arse going to work! (i.e. I'm too lazy to go to work)

"Arsing around" is a popular variation on the above. As you'd expect, this activity involves plenty of sitting on one's arse, not doing a whole lot. Students, workers, and everyone in between are liable to fall into the "arsing around" mode from time to time.

Derogatory Terms

Irish conversation is littered with derogatory terms. You will immediately recognise terms such as "fucker", "bollix" (pron. Bollox), "bitch", and "bastard". Little needs to be said in this regard, other than to illustrate how minor additions may be added to alter their impact.

Take the words "right" and "bad". These may accompany any of the aforementioned terms with devastating effects. For example, a man may be called "a fucker", "a right fucker", or "a bad fucker", with each portraying a different degree of badness. "A right fucker" is usually worse than a mere "fucker", while "a bad fucker" may even be dangerous and should be avoided.

Don't get alarmed if friends call you a "right fecker".

The likelihood is that they are "taking the piss out of you" (i.e. just joking). By the same token, if you are a woman and your friend has just told you of her great new job, you might exclaim with disbelief:

Ye right cow ye!

Gaelic Expressions

Most descriptive of all the derogatory terms are those taken directly from Gaelic. While they are not as popular as they once were, a quick mention is still appropriate because of what they say about Irish sensibilities.

Fools receive a harsh battering: "*an óinseach*" (pron. own-shuk) is a woman with little common sense, and her male counterpart is called "*an amadán*" (pron. om-a-dawn). Foolish behaviour encompasses a wide range of actions but most vivid of all is surely the *"gligín"* (pron. glig-een), a word that translates as "babbler" from Gaelic and aptly describes a giddy personality.

On a more general note, the Gaelic words "*dul*" and "*amú*" are combined to give "*dulamú*" (pron. dul-am-oo), describing one who is going to the dogs. Equally flattering is the term *"cábóg"* (pron.

kaw-bowg, not to be mistaken with cabbage) which translates as a rustic or labourer, but is used to describe one who lacks common courtesy. Conmen also come in for a slating with the description *"goimbín"* (pron. gom-been) being used. In olden times the *goimbín* was a money lender who basically screwed farmers with ruinous interest, but today its usage is broader, and may be applied to anyone who is disliked. The abreviated version *"gom"* will also be heard.

More Recent Additions

Apart from the multitude of Gaelic terms, a scattering of which we've just described, many more have been invented and adapted from elsewhere over the years. In current usage are "langer", "maggot" and "hoor", all of which portray dislikable men. The fool is again heralded with the description *"eejit"*, while the devious man is criticised, perhaps for his unreliability, with the word "bucko". In a similar vein is the wild, energetic, "boyo", possessing the stereotypical male characteristics of aggression and excessive sexual appetite (i.e. with brain firmly rooted between his legs).

Traditionally, the lazy, disorderly woman, known as "a streel", was victim to scathing remarks. Her apparent opposite, the bold, forward-looking, young woman fitted the dubious title of "a strap of a girl". However, the negative attributes of "a streel" and "a strap of a girl" were by no means mutually exclusive. Both might easily be possessed by "the throllop" (i.e. untidy woman, who struck a negative discord in all corners).

Finally, follow the lead of your companion before littering your speech with the above curses. If s/he does not curse at all, think twice before doing so yourself.

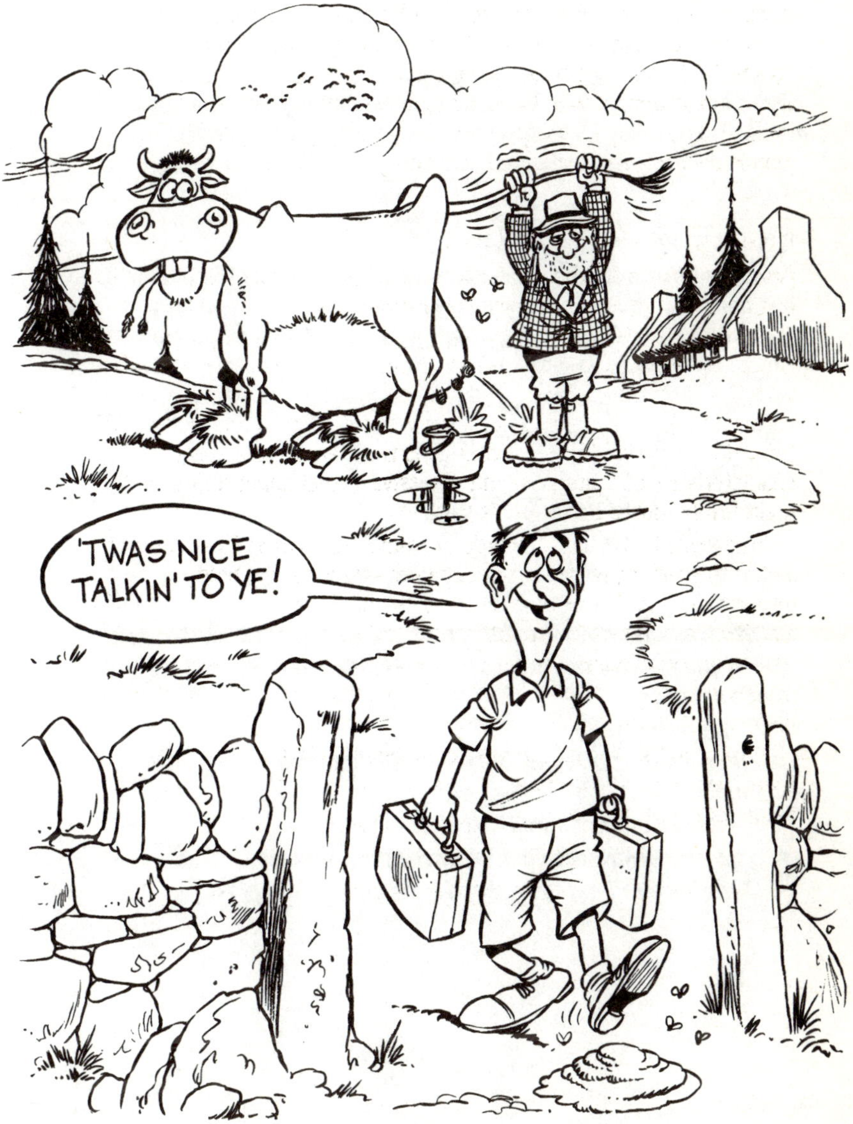
'TWAS NICE TALKIN' TO YE!

PART 5

Parting Shots

FAREWELLS

Well, Lads and Lassies, the cows need milking so it's nearly time to go. Given the fact that this is your sad farewell, you will wish to minimise any regrets that you, or your companions, feel at the thought of parting.

Instead of abruptly announcing "I am leaving!" or "Goodbye", lead up to the inevitable with a few hints:

Is that the time?
Time don't be long passing!
'Tis getting late!
Time is movin' on!

or,

You wouldn't have the time on ye, by any chance?

When you do have to leave, say your goodbyes but also add a touch of touch of hope:

I'll be seeing ye!
I'll be heading off now, but sure I'll bump into you again some time!
I better be off, but sure I'll see you again!

As you move away, cap your farewell with a mumbled:

'Twas nice talking to ye, good luck! and/or *God bless!*

Congratulations

You have just graduated from the Irish Blarney University with top marks. You are now a fully fledged conversational combatant, accomplished in the widest possible range of subjects, from meteorological interpretation to the psychology of the Irish mind.

Due to circumstances beyond our control, we are unable to furnish you with a certificate of course completion at the present time. Nonetheless, your new gift of the gab will make an easy task of convincing employers, family members, and friends, that this course has been completed with due diligence and care.

You are now a valuable member of Irish society. Your talents will be admired, your company sought, and all you meet will hunger for the honey-coated words that flow from your lips. Now, sally forth, confident, upright. Open your mouth and let the world hear.

Good luck! And may ye never be short of something to say!

DICTIONARY

Airlocked
Inebriated

Aisy
Slowly (pron. ay-zee)

Amadán
Fool (pron. om-a-dawn)

Back
West

Bacon
Lump of bacon for boiling

Banjaxed
Broken

Banshee
White-haired old woman of superstitions whose wail forewarns of a death in the family

Batter
On the batter/tear. A drinking spree

Bawneen
Traditional woollen pullover, frequently white in colour

Bean Gárda
Police woman

Begob/Begor
See *Fillers* (page 62)

Below
or Down Below. South

Blaggard
Hoodlum (pron. bla-guard)

Blarney
Bluster, charming chatter

Blather
Incessant chatter

Blond with black skirt
Stout

Bog
Peatland where turf is cut

Bold
Naughty

Bollocking
Scolding

Bollox
or Bollix. Term of abuse

Boreen
A small narrow road

Bother
Trouble or worry

Box
Television

Boycott
Cessation of trade/ communication. Captain Charles Boycott, the 19th century landlord, was the inspiration for, and first victim of, this negotiating tool

Boyo
A wild energetic man

Boys O Boys
Grunted sigh used to punctuate speech. Expression of tiredness

To Bring
To take

Brogue
Irish accent

Bucko
A devious man

Bumper
Fender

Bushed
Exhausted

Carrageen
White edible seaweed

Cat
Very bad

DICTIONARY

Céad Míle Fáilte
One hundred thousand welcomes
(pron. kade mee-la fawl-ta)

Chancer
Devious person. See also *Cute Hoor*

Cheek
Disrespect

Chips
French fries

Ciotóg
Left-handed person. Term of abuse
(pron. kit-ohg)

Clip
Clip on the ear. Painful tug used to punish

Codger
Difficult or irrational individual

Cog
To copy, e.g. in an exam

Colleen
Girl

Come All Ye
Popular folk song or pub song
(pron. come-all-ee)

Contrary
Moody or irritable

Cooreen Caw
Silly person. See also *Ninny Hammer*

Cop On
Common sense

Copper
Small denomination coin

Craic
Fun

Crathur
Poteen, or one deserving pity

Credit
Asset or advantage

Croobeens
Traditional delicacy. Boiled pigs' trotters

Currach
Traditional boat, wicker frame covered with tarred canvas
(pron. kur-uk)

Cute Hoor
Clever or devious man with overriding self-interest. Term often used with sneaking admiration

Daw
Fool

Dead
Extremely, e.g. dead tired

Dead Loss
No good

Deadly
Extremely good or bad

Delph
Cups, plates, saucers, bowls, etc.

Desperate
Very bad

Didder
Hesitancy or agitation

Dig
A physical or psychological blow

Dike
Drain or gully

Dillisk
Edible seaweed

Dirty Job
A bowel movement

Ditch
A fence

DICTIONARY

Divil
Devil. Term of mild abuse used in good-natured fashion

Dollop(s)
A large quantity of something

Dote
An extremely nice child or adult

Dresser
Traditional open display unit for kitchen, holding plates, jugs, etc.

A Drop
A drink

Dry
Thirsty

Dub
Person from Dublin

Dulamu
Male fool (pron. dul-am-oo)

Eejit
Fool

Evening
Anytime after lunch or dinner

To Face
To confront or meet someone

Fag
Cigarette

Fangled
Complicated

Feck
Mild form of fuck

Feck around
To do nothing constructive

Féile
Festival (pron. fay-la)

Fire Away
Continue. Go ahead

Flah
Sexually attractive woman

Fleadh
Feast or festival (pron. flah)

To Flip
To go insane

Fooster
Up in a fooster. Confused or agitated

Football
Gaelic football or soccer

Full
Intoxicated

Gaeltacht
Gaelic-speaking region (pron. Gayle-tukt)

Gabbing
Incessant chatter

Galore
Aplenty

Gárda
Police man

Garsún
Boy (pron. gorsoon)

Gas
Very good

Gawk
To stare at

Gazebo
Tall awkward person

Geansaí
Sweater or pullover (pron. gan-zy)

Get
Bastard. Term of abuse

Gift of the Gab
Noted ability to talk incessantly

Gligín
Fool or giddy person (pron. glig-een)

DICTIONARY

Gob
Mouth

Gobshite
Term of abuse

Goimbín
Conman (pron. gom-been)

Gowl
Disagreeable or ugly person

Grá
Love or fondness, used in song and verse (pron. graw)

Grand
Fine or okay

Greedy gut
Greedy person

Gwawl
Two armfuls of anything

Handy
Convenient

High stool
Bar stool

Holy show
Disgraceful behaviour

Hooley
Party

Hurling
Gaelic team sport

Ignorant
Insensitive or lacking in manners

Irish
Gaelic language

Jackeen
Person from Dublin (viewed with suspicion)

Jar
A drink

Kettle
Electric kettle for boiling water

Kibosh
To end or defeat

Kill
To punish physically or verbally

Kilter
Out of, e.g. Out of order

Kip
Poor or dilapidated accommodation

Knacky
Skilled or creative or resourceful

Langer
Term of abuse

Lash
To go for it or to hit

Laudy Daw
Self-important gobshite

Leg It
To run very fast

Leprechaun
Elf or fairy resembling an old man who is said to possess a crock of gold at the end of a rainbow

Lick up to
To feign affection

Lob
To hit or kick a ball in a high arc

Lump
Lazy Person

Mad
Angry or insane

Maggot
Unpleasant or disgusting character

Maneen
One who strives towards manliness but fails. Mild term of abuse

DICTIONARY

Manky
Dirty or untidy

Manly
Generous or kind-hearted

Mar í dhea
Phrase ending that conveys pretence (pron. mor-ee-ah)

Me
My

Meadhrán
Dizziness (pron. meow-rawn)

Messages
Shopping, e.g. I'm doing the messages

Middling
Fair. Neither good nor bad

Mighty
Excellent

To Mitch
To play truant

Mug
A fool

National school
Primary school

Nicely
Fine, e.g. I'm doing nicely

Ninny Hammer
Silly or giddy individual

Óinseach
Female fool (pron. own-shuk)

Oireachtas
The President and upper and lower houses of Government in the Irish Republic (pron. Er-och-tis)

Ounce
Small Measure e.g. an ounce of sense See *Splink*

Over
East

Pale
Area around Dublin tightly controlled by the English from 12th to 16th centuries. Those living in this area are frequently accused of ignorance when it comes to the affairs of the wider population

Paralatic
Paralytic/intoxicated

Piseóg
Superstition
(pron. pish-ohg)

Piss
Urinate or pour heavily

Plámás
Flatter insincerely
(pron. plau-mauce)

Plank oneself
Settle oneself

Poor Mouth
Complaining mouth

Poteen
Illicit alcoholic beverage

Powerful
Excellent

Press
Cupboard

Púca
Ghost/bogey (pron. poo-ka)

Puck
Hit

Puke
Retch

Pull
Pull a fast one. To get the upper hand by underhand means

DICTIONARY

Puss
Self-pitying facial expression

Quare
Quare hawk or quare fella. Odd or eccentric

Ráiméis
Foolish talk (pron. raw-maysh)

Raise
Anger, e.g. don't raise me with your stories!

Rake of
Large quantity of

Rashers
Thinly sliced bacon for frying

Rear up
Get angry

A ride
A sexually attractive male or female

To ride
To have sexual intercourse

Rí-Rá
Noise or confusion (pron. ree-raw)

Rig Out
Suit of clothes or outfit

Roast
Defeat or scold

Ruaile Buaile
Noise or confusion (pron. Roola Boola) See also *Rí-Rá*

Ruffian
Bully or rowdy male

Salute
Physical act of greeting with a toss of the head

Score
Gaining physical intimacy with a man or woman

Scut
Male who behaves badly

Shanachie
Traditional storyteller

Shanks' Mare
Feet/to walk

Sheebeen
Poteen-making operation or an unlicensed public-house

Shift
See *Score*

Shook
Sick

Show
Give, e.g. show me the book

Sickener
A day of bad weather

Skelp
Take a skelp. To hit someone a blow

To Slag
To tease or make fun of

Sláinte
Health. Traditional Gaelic toast

Sliced Pan
Pre-sliced white bread

Sliotar
Small leather ball used for hurling

Sliver
A thin slice of something

Smig
Chin

Smithereens
Many little pieces, e.g. cup broke into smithereens

Snog
Kiss

Snug
Private compartment in traditional

DICTIONARY

pub

Soakage
Fast-food eating (after drinking)

Soft
Mild and wet

Splink
Splink of sense. Very little sense

Spuds
Potatoes

Strap of
Strap of a girl. Bold and assertive woman

Streel
Disorderly woman or possibly man

String of misery
A miserable person

Sup
A drink

Sure
See *Fillers* (page 62)

Take
Bring, e.g. take the clothes in from the line

Taoiseach
Prime Minister of Irish Republic

T.D.
Member of parliament of Irish Republic (Abr. of *Teachta Dála*)

Tear
To move fast

Thick
Stupid or dull

Throllop
Untidy woman

Toddy
Hot toddy A hot whiskey

Turf
Peat that is cut and dried for fuel

Uisce Beatha
Water of life or whiskey (pron. Ish-ka Ba-ha)

Ullagone
To moan excessively or to be afflicted with self pity

Up
Up or up above. North

Wan
Yer wan. That woman

Wee
Little or small

Whacked
Exhausted

Ye/Yee
You, singular/plural

Yer
That e.g. yer man

Yerra
See *Fillers* (page 62)

Yoke
A thing or contrivance or tool used for performing a task

Other books in the
WIT OF IRELAND Series

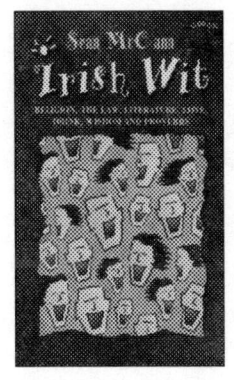

IRISH WIT
Sean McCann

Canny Irish wisdom and proverbs to sum up life – whatever the circumstances. Irish wit is an art form, centuries old yet up-to-the-minute, wise, insulting, obscure, profound and idiotic. The Irish mix wit with wisdom as they do porter and whiskey – and to the same intoxicating effect! In this book, Sean McCann has succeeded in distilling the essence of Irish wit – on love, religion, the 'hard stuff', the English, with help from Behan, Yeats, Swift, Moore and O'Casey. Every kind of utterance, from tongue-in-cheek to foot-in-mouth!

Paperback £4.99/€6.34/$8.95

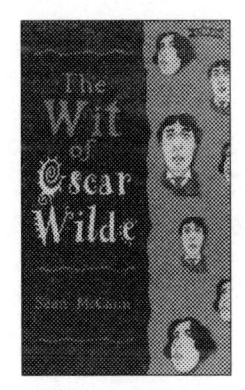

THE WIT OF OSCAR WILDE
Sean McCann

Sean McCann has gathered together the most quoteable, the most memorable and the most useful sayings of that inimitable Irishman, Oscar Wilde. Wilde's genius manifested itself in his plays and poetry, but he is equally famous for his penetrating wit, humour and brilliant repartee. He boasted that he could talk spontaneously on any subject, a claim borne out by the range and scope of the examples in this book.

Paperback £6.50/€7.95/$9.95

DUBLIN WIT
Wisdom, Wickedness, Banter and Bitching
Paul Ryan

Dublin speech and wit is famous all over the world. From the city's greatest writers to the renowned fish, fruit and flower dealers of Moore Street market, wit is the currency of life and the battleground of entertainment. *Dublin Wit* includes exchanges on: love and marriage, pregnancy and romance, fish and fashion, drink, Christmas, neighbours, husbands and children – and, of course, has plenty of insults and threats!

Paperback £5.47/€6.95/$9.95

Send for our full colour catalogue

ORDER FORM

Please send me the books as marked.
I enclose cheque/postal order for £.......... (+£1.00 P&P per title)
OR please charge my credit card ☐ Access/Mastercard ☐ Visa

Card Number __ __ __ __   __ __ __ __   __ __ __ __   __ __ __ __

Expiry Date __ __/__ __

Name............................Tel........................
Address ....
....

Please send orders to: THE O'BRIEN PRESS, 20 Victoria Road, Dublin 6.
Tel: +353 1 4923333; Fax: + 353 1 4922777; E-mail: books@obrien.ie
Website: www.obrien.ie

Note: prices are subject to change without notice